HOW SMALL IS MERCURY?
ASTRONOMY BOOK FOR BEGINNERS
Children's Astronomy Books

BABY PROFESSOR

EDUCATION KIDS

Speedy Publishing LLC
40 E. Main St. #1156
Newark, DE 19711
www.speedypublishing.com
Copyright 2017

In this book, we're going to cover interesting facts about the planet Mercury. So, let's get right to it!

WHAT IS MERCURY?

Mercury is a rocky planet. Of the planets in our Solar System, Mercury is the closest to our Sun, about 36 million miles away at its shortest distance. If you know where to look in the sky, you can see it without using a telescope.

It's one of five planets that are visible to the "naked eye." However, because it's so close to the Sun, it's not easy to observe except during twilight hours or just before the Sun rises.

Every century, Mercury can be observed from Earth as it passes across the face of the Sun. This happens only thirteen times within that one-hundred year period. This event is called a transit, and Mercury is seen as a black pinpoint compared to the Sun. The next transit will take place on November 11, 2019.

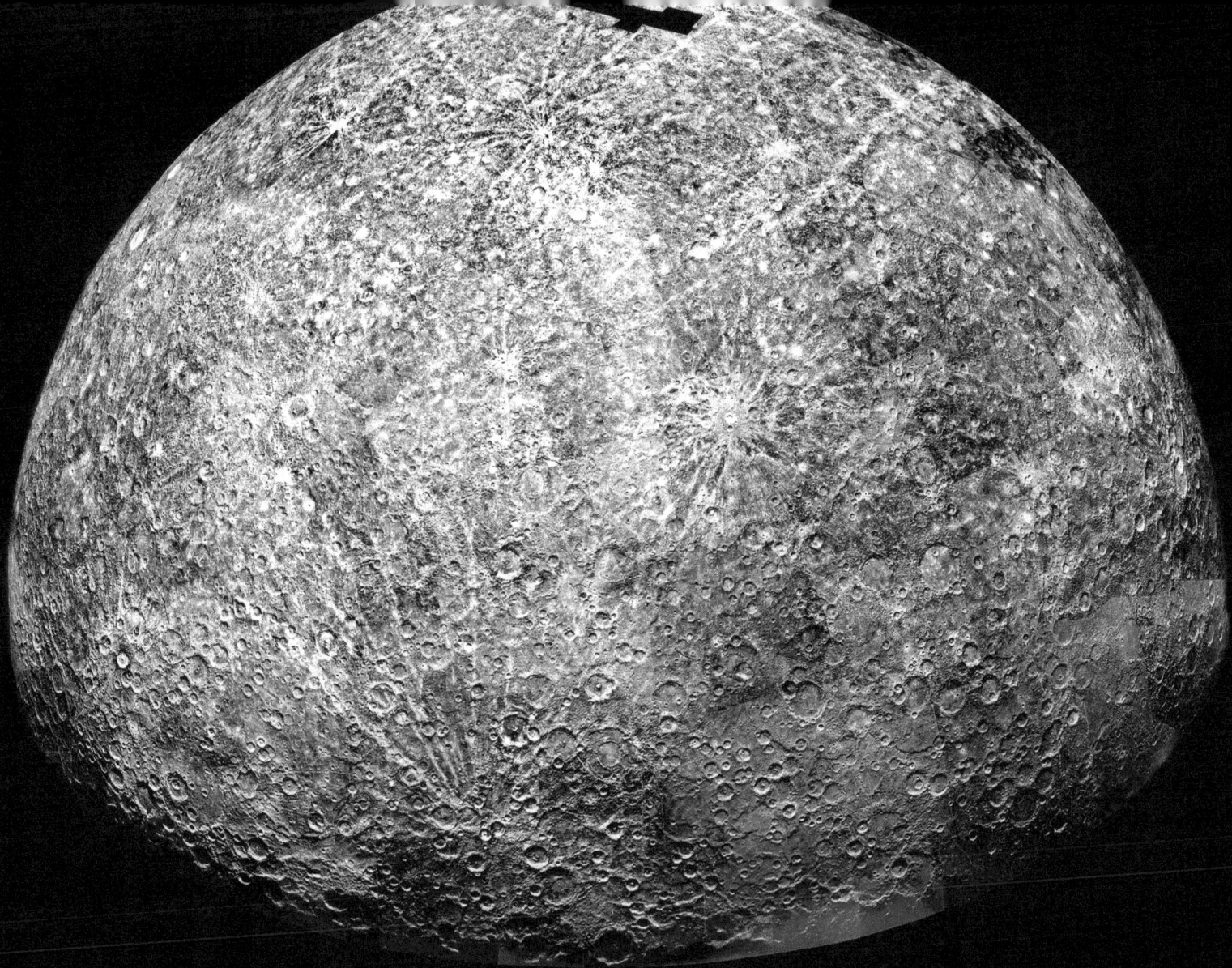

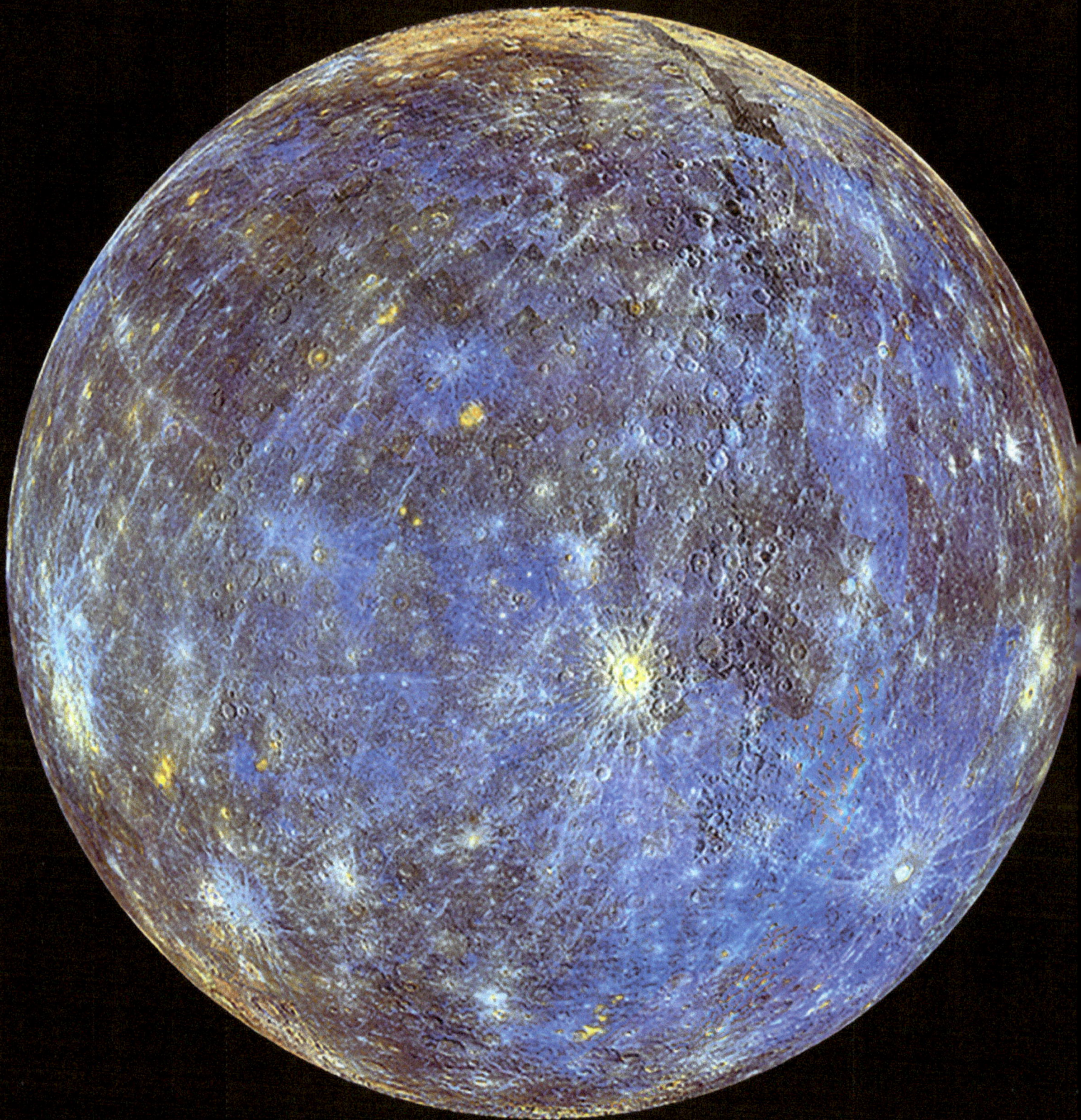

Now that Pluto has been officially declared a "dwarf planet," Mercury is the smallest true planet in our Solar System, followed by Mars, Venus, and Earth it terms of size. It has a diameter of about 4,879 kilometers.

WHAT'S IT LIKE ON THE SURFACE OF MERCURY?

Even though Mercury is the closest planet to the Sun, it's not the hottest planet. The reason is that it has very little atmosphere. Venus is the hottest and this is because the atmosphere there is made of CO_2, which traps the heat and doesn't allow it to escape.

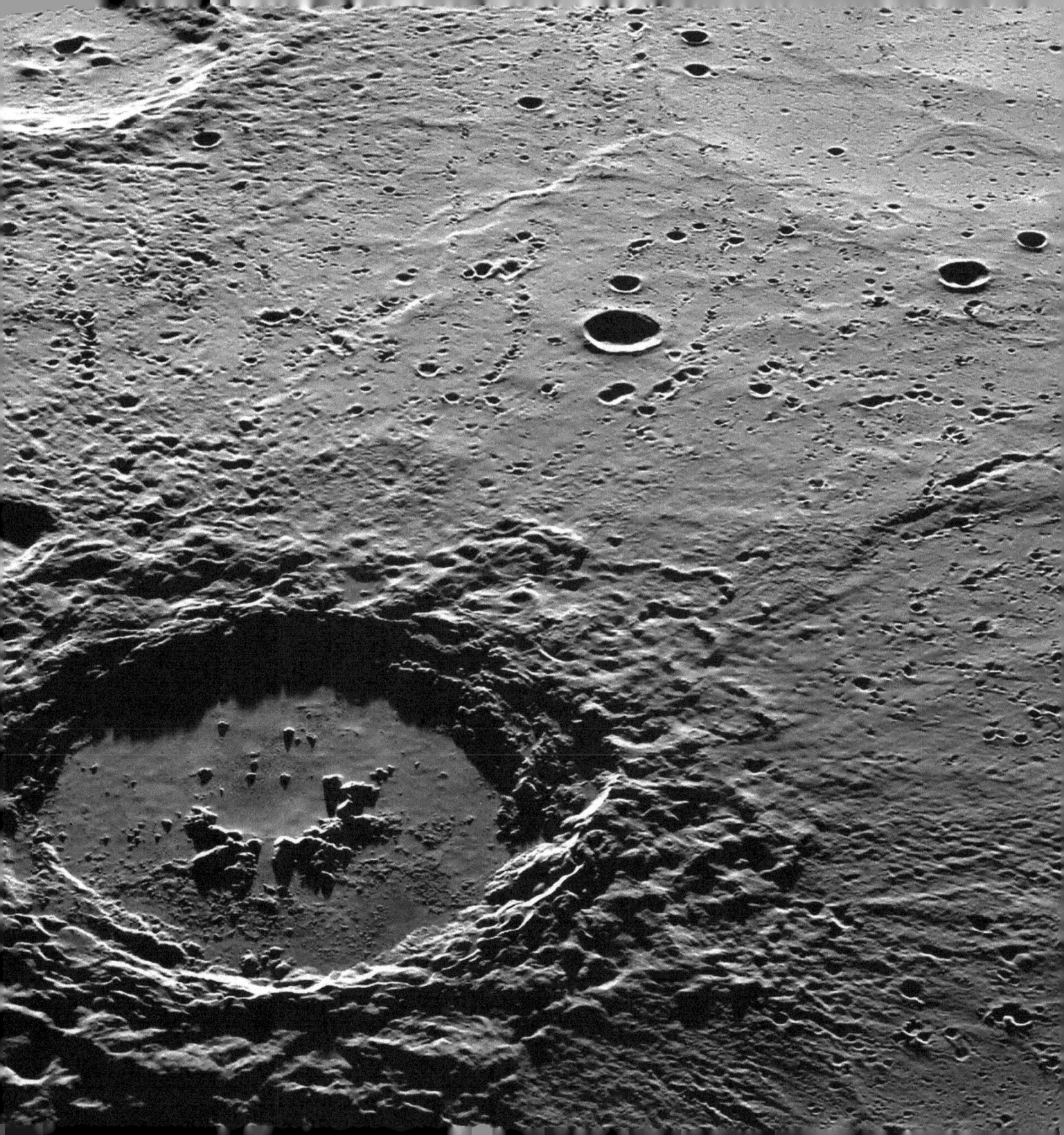

The surface temperature of the planet fluctuates wildly depending on which side is facing the Sun. A high temperature there would be about 800 degrees Fahrenheit and a low temperature would be about minus 280 degrees Fahrenheit.

Mercury has more craters than any other planet in our solar system. They were formed from the impact of both asteroids and comets. Most of its craters have names that

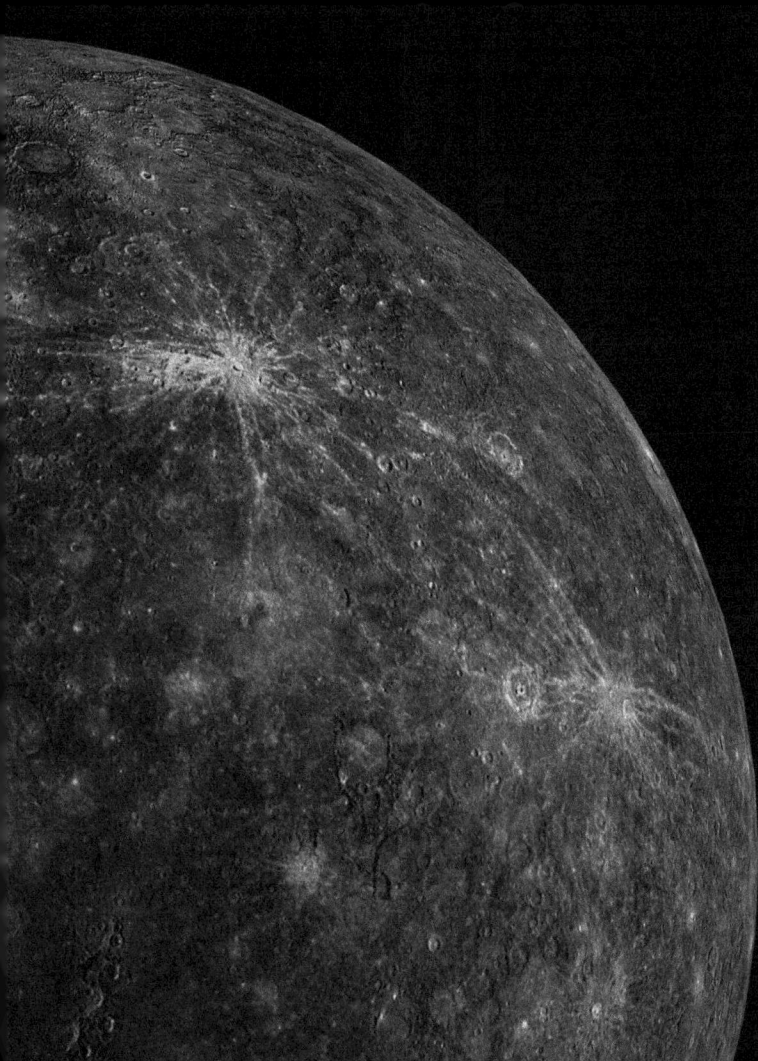

come from famous artists and writers. If a crater is larger than 250 kilometers across, it's referred to as a Basin.

The largest impact crater on the face of the planet is Caloris Basin, which is about 1,550 kilometers wide. It was discovered by Mariner in the 70s. When the asteroid or comet that formed this enormous basin struck, the impact was so forceful that it caused hills to rise from the surface on the other side of the planet!

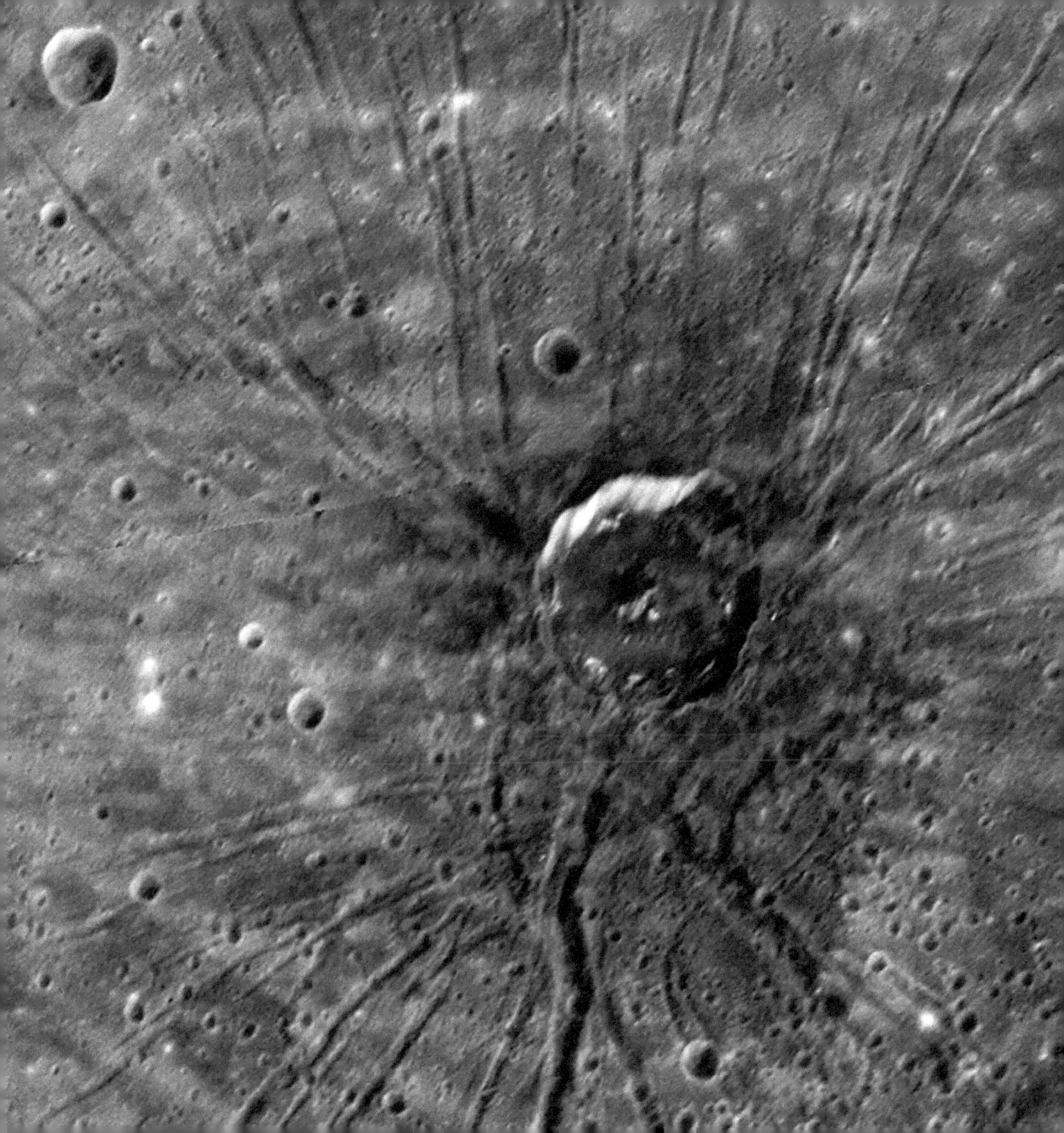

Another interesting feature on the surface of the planet are the Lobate Scarps. Up to a mile in elevation and some several hundred miles long, these are "wrinkles" on the planet's surface. Originally, it was believed that when the planet's iron core cooled, it then contracted, which is what potentially caused this geological feature.

However, within the last few years, NASA scientists have been speculating that the core of Mercury could be molten instead based on data from MESSENGER. More research will be needed to find out. One thing we do know for sure is that the crust is so hard that liquid rock cannot escape to the surface.

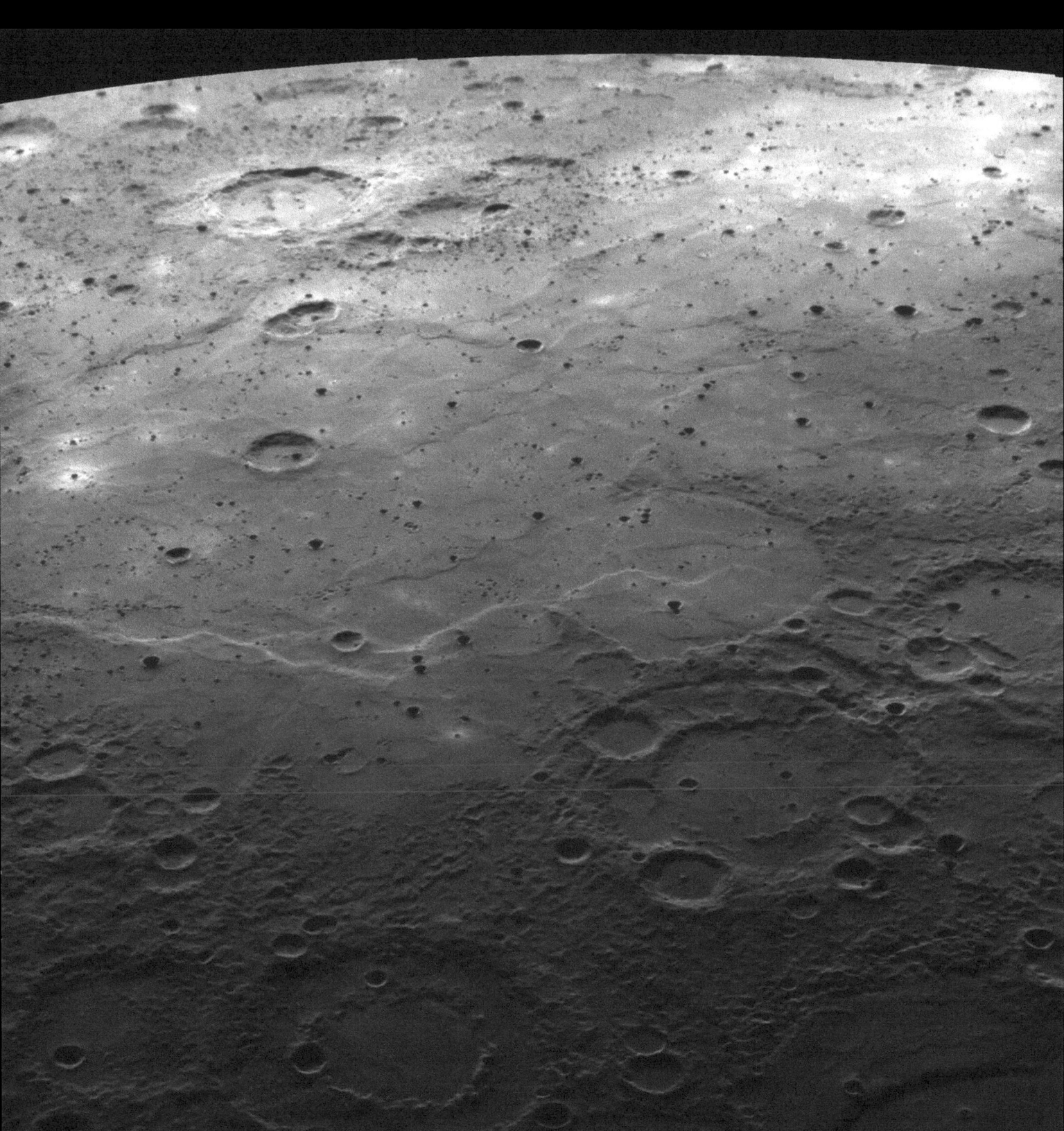

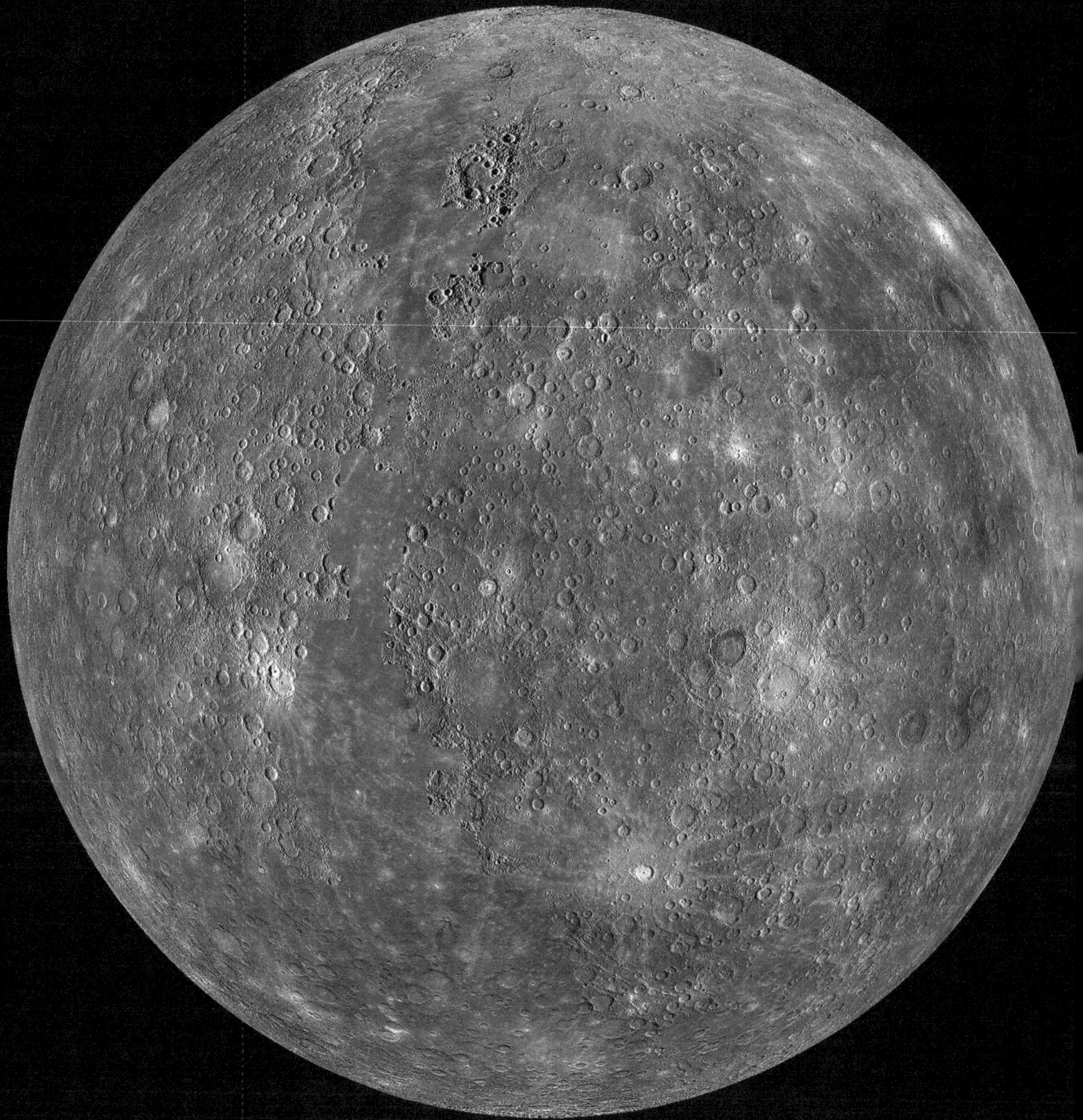

HAVE WE EVER TRAVELED TO MERCURY?

Astronauts have never stepped foot on the surface of Mercury. Of all the planets in our Solar System, Mercury has been the one least explored by spacecraft.

As of 2015, the only unmanned spacecraft that have collected data on the planet were the Mariner 10 probe launched in the 1970s and the MESSENGER, an abbreviation for Mercury Surface, Space Environment, Geochemistry, and Ranging, which was launched in 2004.

Mariner 10

Messenger

The MESSENGER took 6 1/2 years to reach the planet. It continued to obtain scientific information until April of 2015 when it was allowed to crash into the planet's surface. The MESSENGER took over 100,000 photos of the planet.

The spacecraft's goals were to study the planet's chemical composition as well as the history of its geology. It researched the nature of the planet's magnetic field as well as the size and make-up of its core. It was also tasked with studying the gases and composition of the planet's very thin atmosphere, called an exosphere. One of the questions that astronomers are very interested in is why Mercury has a magnetic field while Venus, Mars, and the Moon do not.

Another unmanned craft called the Bepi-Colombo is scheduled to take off for Mercury in October 2018 and arrive there in December of 2025. It's incredibly difficult to launch spacecraft to fly by Mercury, since the

huge gravitational pull of the Sun has to be resisted. This requires the probes to have a large amount of fuel so they can slow down once they get close to the planet.

WHEN WAS MERCURY DISCOVERED?

No one knows exactly when Mercury was discovered. The Sumerians first mentioned the planet in their writings around 3,000 BC. Because the planet's path around the sun was so quick, the Ancient Romans gave it the name "Mercury," after their messenger god with winged feet.

Telescope

In the early 1600s, the astronomer Galileo Galilei was the first person to study the planet through a telescope.

HOW DOES MERCURY COMPARE TO EARTH?

Due to its craters, Mercury is closer in looks to our moon than Earth. If you placed three of the planets the size of Mercury side by side, they would be a little larger than our Earth. Because of this, the gravitational pull on Mercury is much less than that of Earth, which means that if you were able to stand on its surface you would

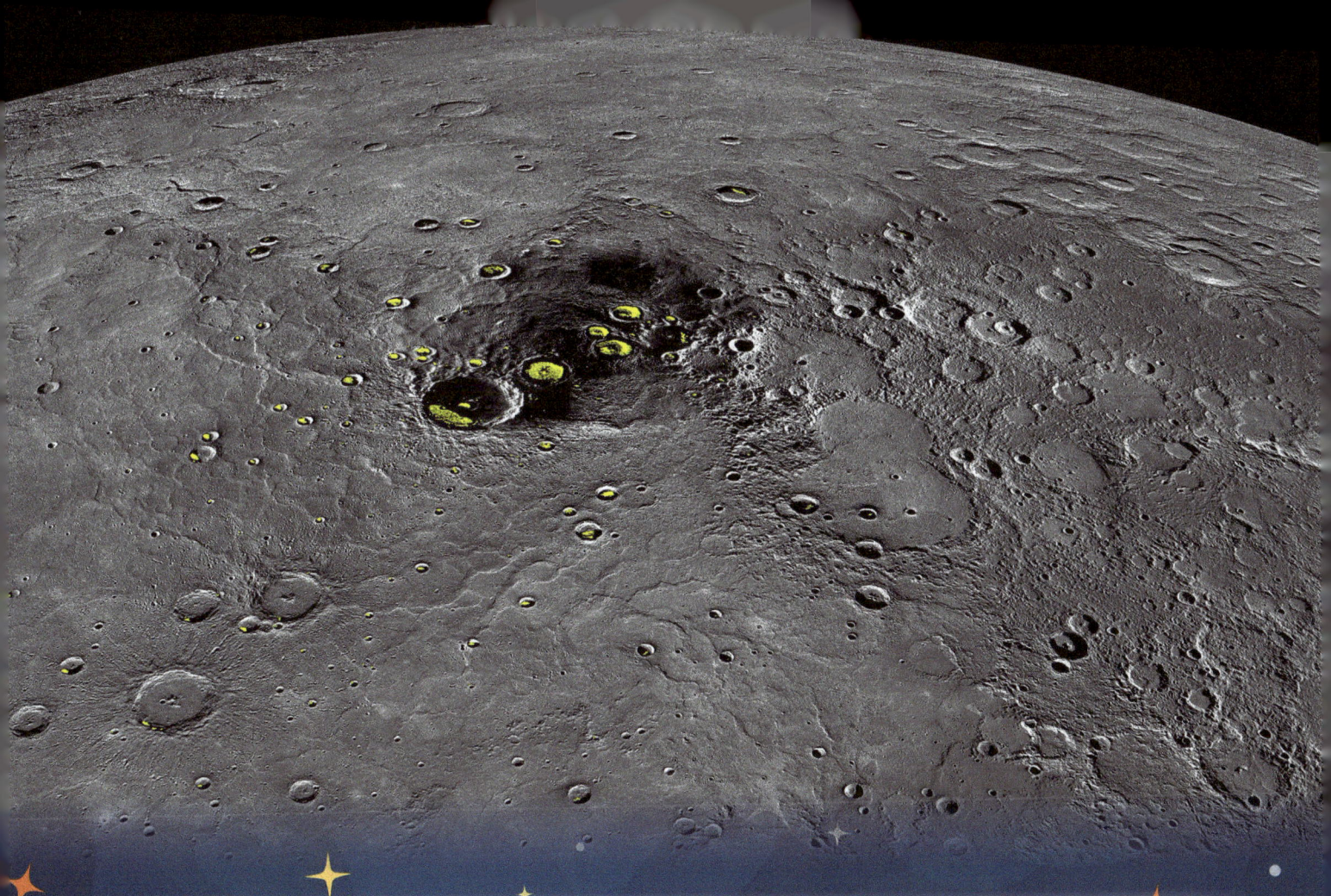

weigh a lot less. For example, if you weigh 100 pounds, on Mercury you would weigh 38% of 100, which is 38 pounds.

Compared to Earth, which is the densest, Mercury ranks second in terms of density when compared to the other planets. It formed a lot differently than the other planets because it was and is so close to the Sun. As the Sun came into its current form, it pushed gas and dust away from itself and the inner Solar System. What it left behind were heavier elements.

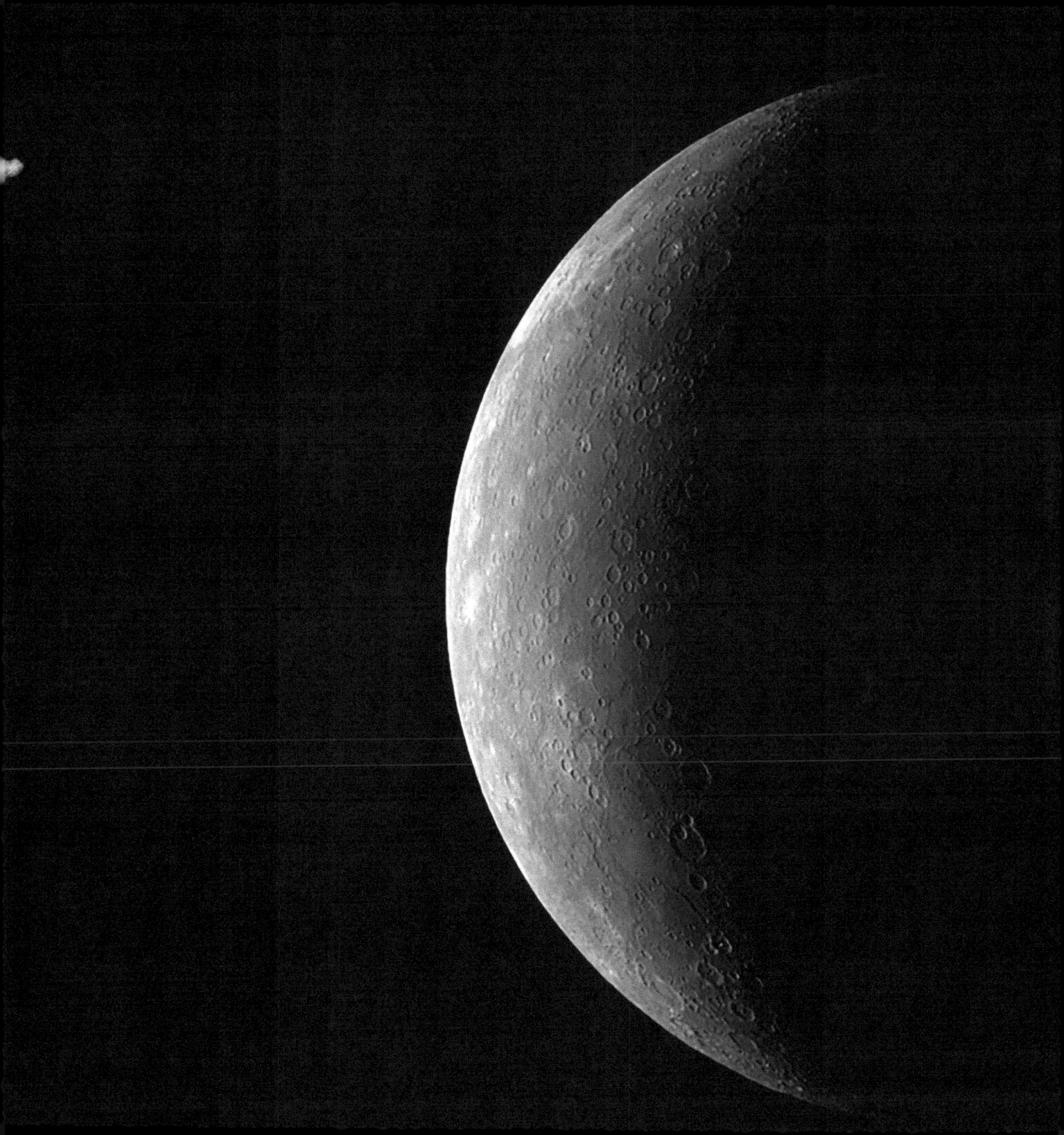

Astronomers believe that Mercury is like a ball made of iron with a thin crust. Its core is very dense and makes up about 75% of the mass of the planet. It has a very thin crust that is about 400 miles or 600 kilometers in thickness.

Mercury is just a little bit larger than Earth's moon and it doesn't have any moons of its own. It is about 5 1/2 % of the mass of Earth.

DAYS AND YEARS ON MERCURY

For a long time, astronomers thought that the same side of Mercury was always facing the Sun, but in 1965 they discovered this wasn't true. Mercury's days are very, very long compared to Earth's. To understand days on Mercury, you'll need to compare a sidereal day to another type of day called a solar day.

A sidereal day is the time that a planet takes to turn on its axis so that the stars are in the same position in the sky. A solar day is the time that a planet takes to turn on its axis so that the Sun appears in the same position. The "day" measurement we typically use is Earth's solar day, which is 24 hours. Earth's average sidereal day is about 23 hours and 56 minutes.

A sidereal day on Mercury lasts a whopping 59 Earth days and its solar day is even longer—176 Earth days! On the other hand, the time it takes Mercury to travel around the Sun, because it's so close, is only 88 days compared to our year, which is 365 days. This means that one year on Mercury takes less time than one day!

Mercury is almost tidally locked with the Sun. This simply means that the time it takes to orbit the sun is getting close to being the same as the time it takes to rotate on its axis. The Moon is an easier example for us to understand. It takes the Moon 28 days to travel around the Earth in orbit. It also takes 28 days for it to rotate once around its own axis. This is why we never see the Moon's dark side from Earth.

If you were able to visit Mercury and stand on its surface, you might see some weird events due to tidal locking. You might see the Sun rise about halfway in the sky. Then, it would reverse its course and then set, all over the course of a one day time period on Mercury.

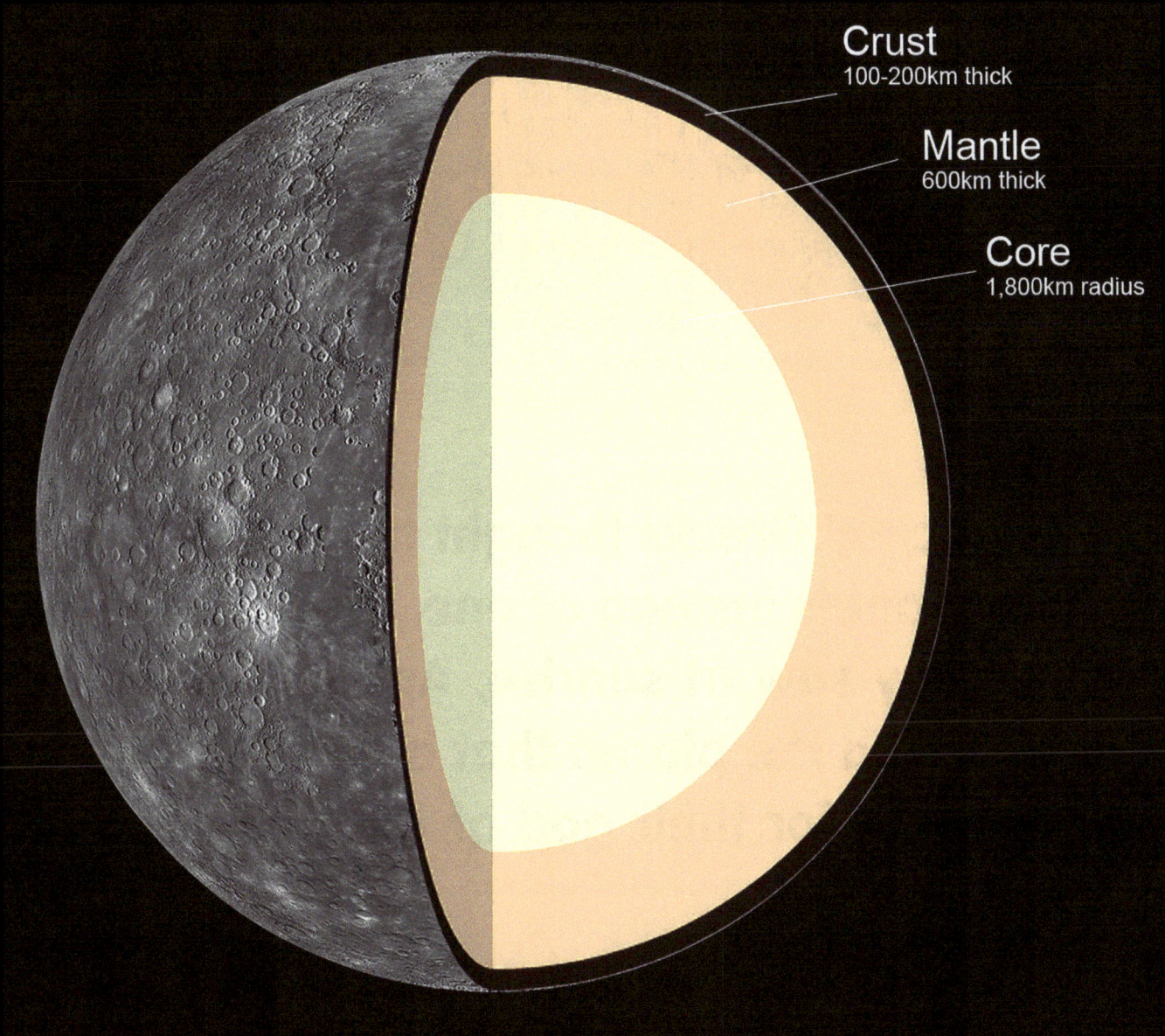

Crust
100-200km thick

Mantle
600km thick

Core
1,800km radius

FASCINATING FACTS ABOUT MERCURY

The Ancient Greeks thought that Mercury was two planets instead of one. They named the planet they saw at sunrise, Apollo, after their sun god, and the planet that appeared at sunset, Hermes, for their god of the underworld.

Mercury orbits the Sun at a quicker pace than any other planet in the Solar System.

Mercury also refers to a chemical element. Alchemists once thought that it would be possible to create gold from mercury.

Mercury's orbit is the least round of all the planet's orbits. Its eccentric orbit means that it ranges in distance from 46 million kilometers to 70 million kilometers from the Sun.

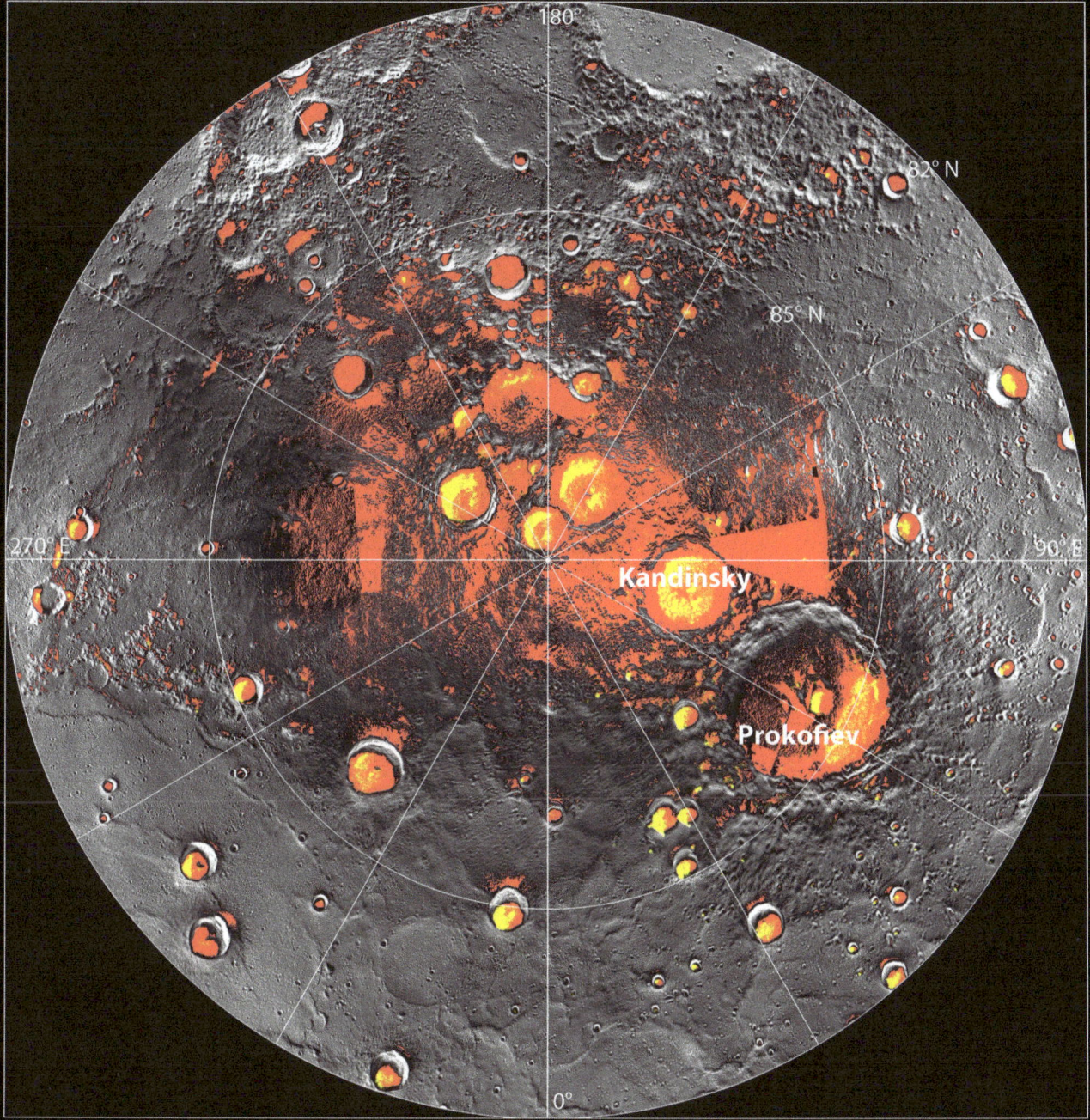

Awesome! Now you know more about the planet Mercury, the smallest planet in our Solar System. You can find more Astronomy books from Baby Professor by searching the website of your favorite book retailer.

Visit

BABY PROFESSOR
EDUCATION KIDS

www.BabyProfessorBooks.com

to download Free Baby Professor eBooks
and view our catalog of new and exciting
Children's Books

9 798869 417077